When My Brother Went to Prison

KIDS HAVE *TROUBLES* TOO

When My Brother Went to Prison

by Sheila Stewart and Rae Simons

PUBLISHERS

Mason Crest Publishers

MASON CREST PUBLISHERS INC.
370 Reed Road
Broomall, Pennsylvania 19008
(866)MCP-BOOK (toll free)
www.masoncrest.com

First Printing
9 8 7 6 5 4 3 2 1

CIP on file with the Library of Congress

ISBN (set) 978-1-4222-1691-0   ISBN 978-1-4222-1695-8
ISBN (ppbk set) 978-1-4222-1904-1   ISBN (ppbk) 978-1-4222-1908-9

Design by MK Bassett-Harvey.
Produced by Harding House Publishing Service, Inc.
www.hardinghousepages.com
Cover design by Torque Advertising + Design.
Printed in USA by Bang Printing.

The creators of this book have made every effort to provide accurate information, but it should not be used as a substitute for the help and services of trained professionals.

Introduction

Each child is unique—and each child encounters a unique set of circumstances in life. Some of these circumstances are more challenging than others, and how a child copes with those challenges will depend in large part on the other resources in her life.

The issues children encounter cover a wide range. Some of these are common to almost all children, including threats to self-esteem, anger management, and learning to identify emotions. Others are more unique to individual families, but problems such as parental unemployment, a death in the family, or divorce and remarriage are common but traumatic events in many children's lives. Still others—like domestic abuse, alcoholism, and the incarceration of a family member—are unfortunately not uncommon in today's world.

Whatever problems a child encounters in life, understanding that he is not alone is a key component to helping him cope. These books, both their fiction and nonfiction elements, allow children to see that other children are in the same situations. The books make excellent tools for triggering conversation in a nonthreatening way. They will also promote understanding and compassion in children who may not be experiencing these issues themselves.

These books offer children important factual information—but perhaps more important, they offer hope.

—*Cindy Croft, M.A., Ed., Director of the Center for Inclusive Child Care*

The pounding woke me up. My room was still dark and I didn't know what time it was. I heard somebody walking down the hall, the front door opening, and then voices. More footsteps. The voices got loud. I sat up and got out of bed.

The light was on in the hall and my mom was a couple of steps ahead of me, tying the belt of her robe as she walked toward the front door. My dad stood at the front door talking to two police officers, one a man and one a woman.

"He's not here," Dad was saying. "He went out with some friends last night and he wasn't back when I went to bed. I don't know if he came home at all or not."

Chris. They were talking about Chris, my nineteen-year-old brother.

"What happened to Chris?" Mom sounded scared.

"We don't know that anything happened to him, ma'am," the woman officer said. "We just need to talk to him about an incident that occurred earlier this evening."

"What kind of incident?" Mom asked.

The woman didn't answer her, and instead gave Dad a business card. "If he comes back, tell him to call me. It will look better for him if he comes in voluntarily."

Dad took the card slowly and we all stared at the two officers.

"Are you going to arrest him?" I asked, but they ignored me too and left instead.

For a couple of seconds, nobody said anything, and then Dad looked at me. "Go back to bed, Thomas," he said.

"But—" I started, but he cut me off.

"Bed. Now."

I'd never seen Dad look so upset, and Mom was starting to cry. Suddenly, I didn't want to ask questions anymore. I wanted to go to bed and go to sleep and wake up to find out this was just a bad dream. I wanted Chris to be there and tell me everyone was just being silly.

My sister Ashley opened her door as I walked back down the hall to my room. Her hair was sticking up on one side, and her face had pillow creases on it. Ashley was fifteen and didn't usually come out of her room until she looked perfect, so I wasn't used to seeing her like this.

"What's going on?" she asked.

"Chris is in trouble," I said.

"What happened? Is he okay?"

Dad saw us and waved his arm at us. "Everybody go back to bed!" He wasn't yelling, not quite. "We'll talk about it in the morning."

Back in bed, I thought I wouldn't be able to sleep at all. What could Chris have done? I wondered. He'd been in trouble with Mom and Dad before, but he'd never had the police come looking for him in the middle of the night. Somehow, I finally fell asleep.

When I woke up the next morning, I didn't remember right away what had happened in the night. I had an awful feeling that something was wrong, though. I heard the phone ring down the hall, and then I remembered.

It was a Saturday morning, so usually I would have just rolled over and gone back to sleep for a while, but instead I got up and went down to the kitchen. Mom was sitting at the table, her hands over her face and her elbows on the table. Dad was talking on the phone. He looked very, very tired.

I got myself a bowl of cereal and sat down, but I didn't feel hungry enough to eat. Instead, I just watched Dad. He wasn't saying much, mostly just listening. Ashley came out after another few minutes, and Dad was still on the phone.

Finally, he hung up. We all looked at him, waiting for him to tell us what was going on.

"We need to go now," Dad said to Mom. "The lawyer will meet us at the police station."

"What happened to Chris?" Ashley asked.

"He got himself arrested," Dad said.

"What did he do?" I asked. My voice wouldn't work and it came out as a whisper.

Dad sighed. "He was selling drugs at a party. Ecstasy. One of the kids had a seizure." He stopped

talking because Mom had started sobbing. I had never heard Mom cry like that. It was awful. I wanted to run out of the room and bury my head under my pillow.

After Mom and Dad left to go to the police station, Ashley and I looked at each other.

"He's such an idiot," Ashley said finally. She stood up and stalked down the hall to her room, slamming her door behind her.

I went into the living room and turned on the TV. I sat on the couch and flicked through the channels, over and over again. I was not going to think about Chris. I was not going to think about Mom crying. I was not going to think about anything. My brain wouldn't focus on the shows I kept watching bits of, but I didn't care. At least they blocked out some of the other stuff I was not going to think about.

I sat in front of the TV all day. I didn't even get dressed. I didn't eat anything. I was hungry and not hungry at the same time. My stomach got nervous and twitchy if I tried to think at all, so I kept not thinking and flicking through channels.

It was almost dark out when Mom and Dad got home, but they had Chris with them. I jumped up as soon as I saw him and ran to throw my arms around him. He hugged me back and ruffled my hair, but he didn't say anything. All of a sudden, I wanted to hit him. I wanted to punch him and kick him and scream at him. But I didn't. Instead, I hugged him harder and harder, like I was going to squeeze him in half and my hugging was almost like hitting.

"Um, Thomas," Chris said. "I can't breathe. Do you think you could loosen your grip a little?"

So I let go. And then I ran down the hall to my room. Ashley passed me in the hall. Right before I slammed my door, I heard her yell, "You jerk!" and I heard the sound of her hand slapping Chris's face. I guess she must have felt the same way I did.

I lay on my face on my bed and cried and cried. I hadn't cried like that in years, not since I was a little kid. Everything was so messed up and wrong.

On Monday, I didn't want to go to school, but Dad made me. He said life had to go on. He and Mom both went to work, and Ashley and I went to school. Chris went back to college and to his job at the grocery store, too. It was like life really had gone back to normal, except that nothing was quite right and it really wasn't normal at all.

At school, I didn't know what to say to anybody. I couldn't tell them what had happened to Chris. I didn't want to talk about it. I didn't want anybody to know. But, because that was all I was thinking about a lot of the time, I didn't say much at all. My friends didn't know what was wrong with me. I started getting bad grades, so then my teachers didn't know what was wrong with me either.

At home, nobody talked much either. Nobody laughed. Ashley stayed in her room most of the time. Chris was always having to go to court or meet with the lawyer. Mom and Dad went with him, but they wouldn't let me go.

A few weeks later, my teacher, Ms. Blaney, called me up to her desk.

"What's going on, Thomas?" she asked. She had the math test we'd done yesterday on her desk and I could see the red "42" written at the top and circled. I'd never done that badly on anything before.

I shrugged. I couldn't think of anything to say.

"You've always been a good student," she said. "Clearly, something is going on. I'm going to need to call your parents, you know."

I shrugged again, and she sighed. I didn't want her to call Mom and Dad, but I still couldn't make myself talk to her. I couldn't make the words, "My brother sold drugs and now he's going to prison," come out of my mouth.

I thought she would wait until that evening to call my parents, but she must have called during lunch, because she called me up to her desk again that afternoon.

"You could have told me about your brother," she said. "I understand that you're upset and this is hard to deal with. I've arranged a meeting with your parents and the school counselor tomorrow afternoon. You're going to get through this, Thomas."

"Okay," I said, but what I was really thinking was, Oh, great. Because I didn't want to have a meeting. I didn't want people to try to deal with me.

I walked back to my seat and saw Deanna, who sat closest to Ms. Blaney's desk, staring at me. I hoped she hadn't heard anything Ms. Blaney said.

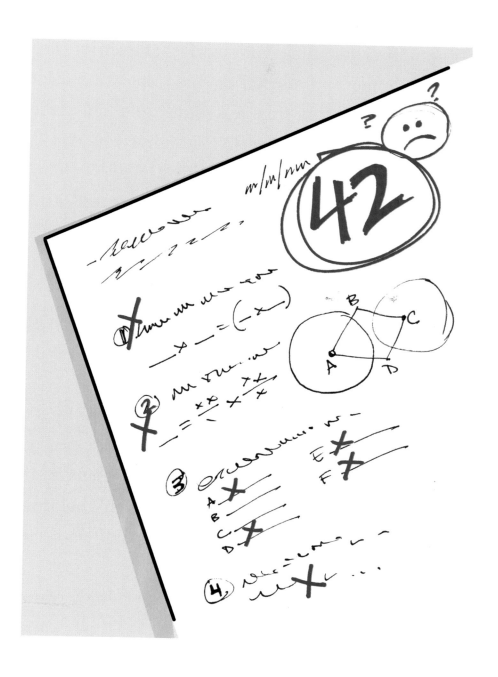

When Mom got home from work that evening, she looked at me and started crying. She cried a lot these days, but this time it was me who had made her cry, and that was horrible. I realized suddenly, too, just how awful she was looking lately, with big dark circles under her eyes. She had gotten skinnier too, and she felt bony when she hugged me.

"I'm so sorry, Thomas," she said. "You're supposed to be having fun and enjoying your life. I know this isn't any easier for you than the rest of us. And you're only ten once." She tried to smile at me, but it didn't quite work.

Dad wasn't quite as sympathetic when he got home. "Your mother doesn't need another son to worry about," he said to me. "I suppose it's natural that you want attention too, but this isn't helping anything. The trial starts next week, and we need all our energy for that."

"I don't want attention," I said. "I don't want you to go to the meeting at school. I just want everything to go back to the way it used to be."

Dad stared at me for a second, and then he just grabbed me and hugged me. "I'm sorry, Thomas," he said, and I had a horrible feeling that he was crying too. I wished I'd never seen my parents cry.

After supper, I was in my room, trying to work on my homework, when I heard a crash from Chris's room on the other side of the wall. I hadn't talked to Chris very much since he'd been arrested. I felt weird around him, like I didn't know what to say, and that maybe he was really a different person than I'd thought. I didn't ignore him all the time, though, like Ashley did.

I got up and went over to Chris's room to see what the crash was. I was kind of afraid he'd taken some drugs and had a seizure, like the person at the party that had started this whole thing.

When I opened the door, I saw Chris sitting on the edge of his bed, his hands over his face, rocking back and forth. Broken glass was all over the rug. It looked like one of the glasses from the kitchen.

I started to back out of the room, but Chris must have heard the door. He stopped rocking, and looked at me over the top of his fingers.

"Come in, Thomas," he said.

I didn't know what to say, so I just stood there in the doorway.

"I've pretty much messed everything up, haven't I?" he said. He took his hands down from his face. "I had no idea, you know that? I mean, yeah, I knew it was illegal and a bad idea and all that, but I didn't really know. . . ." He paused, and then he said, "My lawyer says they might send me to prison for two or three years. But if something worse had happened, like if that girl had died when she had a seizure, it would be a minimum of twenty years, just like that."

I couldn't even think what twenty years in prison meant. It was twice as long as I'd been alive. I finally went all the way into the room. I knelt down on the floor and started picking up the broken glass. I didn't know what else to do to make things better.

"Thomas . . ." Chris said, and then stopped. "I wish I'd been a better brother," he said finally.

I dropped the pieces of glass in the wastebasket and looked at him. "You are a good brother," I said. "Everybody messes up, but you're still a good brother."

I tried to get Dad to let me go to Chris's trial, but he said I had to go to school. I wanted to be there for him, but I heard Mom tell Dad she didn't want me to hear the things they were going to say about Chris.

The trial only took two days. I thought it would be longer, because on movies trials seem like they take weeks and weeks. On the second day, Mom and Dad came home without Chris. Mom's eyes and the end of her nose were very red.

"Where's Chris?" I asked, even though I was pretty sure I knew.

"The trial's over," Dad said. "The judge sentenced him to thirty months. They took him into custody right away."

"How much is thirty months?" I asked, trying to work it out. I thought at first that it wouldn't be as long as Chris had said, since it was in months instead of years, but then Dad said, "Two and a half years."

That seemed like a really long time to me.

"When can we go visit him?" I asked.

"I don't know," Dad said. "We'll see."

Mom and Dad didn't end up letting me go see Chris for over a month. Visiting day was in the middle of the week, so I would have to miss school. Dad and the school counselor agreed that I could visit Chris when my grades got back up, so that gave me a reason to try to do well.

Before that, though, the thing I had been worried about happened at school: People found out what had happened to Chris.

It happened right after the trial. Maybe it was on the news or the Internet or something.

I was in the hall before class and Deanna walked by me with her friends.

"There's that criminal's brother," she said loudly. "I'll bet he's a druggie like his loser brother."

I felt my face get all hot, but I didn't look at her and I didn't say anything.

After that, people were always talking about it and bugging me about it. I hated it. Even some of my friends bugged me about it. The only person who was completely nice about it was my best friend Luis. I was glad I had him.

On the day I finally got to go see Chris, we had to get up and leave pretty early. The prison was almost an hour away, and Dad said there were always a lot of people waiting to visit their families. Ashley wasn't going, but she'd agreed she'd go in two weeks. She was still mad at Chris, but I thought she might forgive him soon.

We drove into the parking lot and I looked at the big gray building and the high fences with lots and lots of curly wire at the top. I wished Chris didn't have to be here, that he could just come home.

When we went in, Dad gave the guard a bunch of papers and we all had to walk through a metal detector. The man in front of us kept setting off the metal detector, so they finally gave him some other clothes to change into so he could try again. I was worried that we would set off the metal detector too, but none of us had a problem.

We went into another room, where we had to wait until they called our names. Lots of other people were sitting around waiting too. There were a few kids, mostly babies or really little kids, but most people were grownups. The babies and kids just cried or ran around like they weren't in some weird place. I wished I could be like that.

After a long time, they called our names and we went into another room. People were sitting at tables all over a big room and guards were walking around. I looked around and finally saw Chris sitting at a table halfway across the room. He waved when he saw me look at him.

Chris hugged us when we got to his table and then sat down again.

"It's good to see you," he said to me. He looked better than the last time I'd seen him, which made me feel a little better.

"Is it bad here?" I asked.

"You know all the horrible things you see about prison on TV?" he said.

"Yeah. . ."

"It's not anywhere near that bad," he said, and smiled at me. "It's not great, but I'll survive. I'm going to do my time and then I'm never looking back. I'm going to be someone who makes you all proud of me again."

"Good." I smiled back at him. "Because I miss you."

I still didn't feel good about Chris being in prison. But at least now I had something to look forward to—the day when Chris would come home.

Who Has a Brother in Prison?

There are over two and a half million people in prison in the United States. That's one out of every one hundred adults. And like everyone else, most people in prison have families—a husband or wife, kids, mothers, grandmas, brothers and sisters—and friends, too. Think about all the people who know and love these two and a half million people in prison! There are millions and millions of them. You are not alone if you have a brother or somebody else in your family in jail. There are millions of kids like you all over America.

Why Did This Happen?

Prison is a place where people get sent as a punishment for doing something wrong, something that is against the law, something that is called a crime.

You've probably done something wrong at least a few times in your life, and maybe it was bad enough that you got in trouble for doing it, and your mom or your babysitter or your teacher decided you had to be punished. Maybe you got sent to your room, or weren't allowed to go to the movies with your friend, or maybe you couldn't use your computer during the

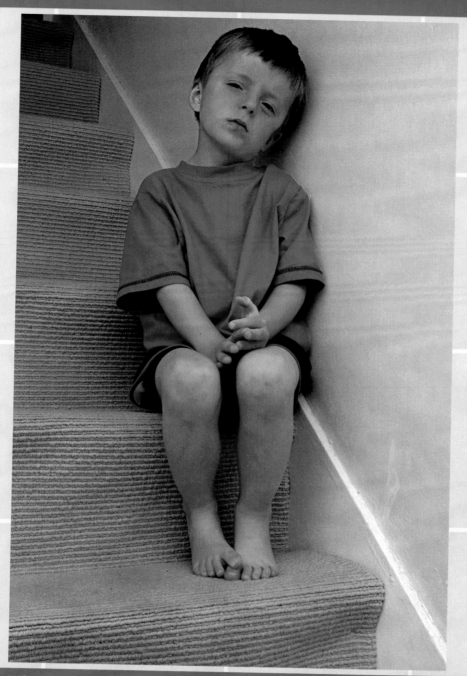

When children disobey their parents, they are sometimes sent to sit on the stairs for a while. It's not the same as prison, but they are both consequences for doing something wrong.

Prisons can look scary, because they are made to keep people inside.

time you were being punished. A lot of kids, when they get in trouble, are told that they are being punished "for your own good" and to "teach you a lesson." That's because when grownups punish a child, they are doing it so that the child really understands they did something wrong, something that will get them in trouble every time they do it—and so that they will remember to not do it again!

Getting sent to prison is pretty much the same idea. A grownup does something against the **law**, the police see it or find out about it and arrest him, a judge decides he needs to be punished and learn a lesson—and prison is the punishment.

Since most people in prison today are there because of crimes that have to do with drugs, maybe the police caught your older brother trying to sell drugs and arrested him. Everyone, including your brother, knows that drugs are bad and that selling drugs is against the law, but your brother did it. That was wrong. If it was a big crime, the police might take your brother to jail right away, but that's really only so that the police know exactly where he is when it is time for him to

> ### *Understand the Word*
>
> A **law** is a rule made by a city, a state, or a country, that everyone living there is supposed to obey.

go to trial. A trial is where people called lawyers (who know all about the law), and a judge (who works for the city, state, or country that made the law)—and sometimes a group of people called a jury—will come together to decide if your brother really did something against the law, and if he did, what his punishment should be. The amount of time the judge decides your brother has to spend in prison as a punishment for what he did is called a "sentence."

What Goes on in Families

Having someone they love arrested, having a trial, and getting sentenced by a judge to prison is a very, very hard time for a family. Everyone in the family, grownups and kids, may feel sad about what happened and afraid of what's going to happen next. Grownups may be talking about all kinds of things that you don't understand—like lawyers and pleas and bail—your parents may be very angry at your brother, or blame the judge or your brother's friends for him having to go to prison. There may be yelling, there may be crying. Your mom might blame your dad for what your brother did, Grandma may be very angry at your parents for letting this happen.

And all of a sudden, someone who was a part of your family is gone. The family has to figure out how to live without having him around, and having him in prison—a place that can be very scary. Sometimes people can feel ashamed and embarrassed about having someone in their family in prison and it can be very hard for them, but your family should try to remember they are not alone: millions of people are going through the same thing. Some prisons, churches,

At the trial, the judge will listen to what everyone has to say and then make his ruling. If it is a jury trial, the jury will decide whether the person is guilty and then the judge will decide what the sentence should be.

and communities run groups where family members of **inmates** can get together and talk about how they are feeling and support each other. Having support outside of the family can help a lot.

What About You?

Kids sometimes blame themselves when bad things happen in their family, so you need to remember it's not your fault that your brother is in prison. You probably love your older brother and maybe you always looked up to him because he was so big and cool and exciting to be around. It's natural for you to feel sad that he got in trouble, to miss him while he's in jail, maybe even to be a little mad at him for what he did. Yes, your brother did something wrong, maybe even something that you know is really bad, like hurting somebody, but he is still your brother. It may be hard, and it may take a while, but if you love someone, it's good to try to forgive him for the bad thing that he did—and, if you can, help him to not do it again. Your brother made a mistake and he's being punished for it, but it's not wrong for you to love him.

Understand the Word

People who are living in prison are called **inmates**.

You may not want to talk to people outside of your family about your brother in prison. But sometimes you may feel so sad or so afraid for your brother that you need to tell someone who cares about you how you feel so you can get help with your feelings. It may really be a good thing for your teacher or your good friend to know about what you and your family are going through. A lot of people are nice and

Talking to an adult can help you make sense out of what you are feeling.

Inmates at prisons sometimes participate in work crews. Thomas' brother Chris, in this story, might work with other prisoners to pick up garbage along the side of a highway, for example.

understanding, and a lot of kids and grownups, millions of them, are going through the same thing you are.

And remember, don't think because your brother went to prison that it's a cool thing to do, or something you would ever want to do yourself! Being in prison is a punishment, and it's not a nice place to be. Most prisons are crowded and dirty places. Your brother lives in a small room called a cell and spends most of his time there. He does not have the freedom to do what he wants when he wants to. His meals (and the food is usually pretty bad in prison), his recreation time, just about every minute of his day, are all watched over by prison guards and take place in a crowd of other inmates.

Prison also try to help people who have done something wrong learn the **skills** that will help them be better, happier people and live better lives when they get out. Many people get treatment to quit drugs and alcohol while they are in prison. Many prisons have schools where inmates can continue their education or learn how to do jobs so they can earn money when they get out. Prison really can be a GOOD thing if an

> ### Understand the Word
>
> **Skills** are things you are able to do, like reading or writing or knowing how to use a computer.

inmate wants to better himself and learn how to stay out of trouble in the future.

What You Can Do to Help Your Brother in Prison

Your brother misses you and your family and it's important for you—and for him—to stay in touch. You can write him letters, send him pictures you've drawn, or greeting cards just to let him know you miss him. He may be allowed to call home, or have his family call him, and he'll probably be really happy just to hear

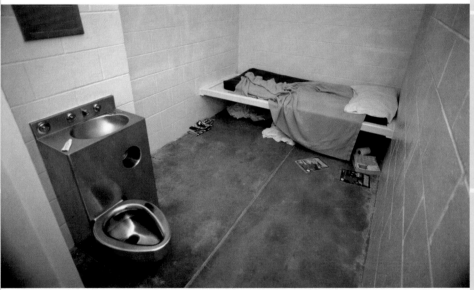

Prison cells aren't usually very comfortable, but they have a bed, a toilet, and a sink, and inmates can have a few books or magazines.

your voice. Try to let him know that you love him. Tell him you hope he's doing things and learning things in prison that will help him when he gets out.

A grownup may take you to visit your brother in prison. You will probably feel excited about having the chance to see your brother, but you may also be nervous. Some prisons have special busses to take families of inmates to the prison for visiting day, or maybe you'll go by car or a regular bus. Most prisons are big ugly buildings surrounded by tall fences. You and the grownups you're with will be searched to make sure you're not bringing anything into the prison you're not allowed to, and you'll probably go through a metal detector, too. There will be a lot of guards in uniform around (they look like police officers), probably with guns and clubs, and they might seem kind of scary (but they won't hurt you!). The prison will probably not smell very good.

Most inmate family visits take place in a big noisy room where people sit at tables and talk with each other. The room will be filled with lots of people and there will probably be little kids crying and people talking loud, maybe speaking a language you don't understand. Just try to remember that everyone is there for the same reason, to visit with someone they love whom they don't get to see very often. Your brother will probably look different than you remember him. He'll be wearing a prison uniform, and he may have lost weight because of the bad food. Then again, if he was on drugs when he was arrested, he may look healthier and better than he did the last time you saw him! The other inmates may seem scary to you, but nobody will let anything bad happen to you when you're there.

The visit won't be long, probably an hour at most, and if you're visiting with a big family group you might not have a lot of time to talk with your brother. You may feel funny or shy or not in the mood to talk. The important thing is you're together. He's still your brother, and you love him—and he loves you.

Your brother broke the law, had a trial, and went to prison. He did something wrong, maybe something you know was bad, but he is being punished for it and hopefully learning something in prison that will help him be a better person when he gets out. No person is all bad, and every person, as long as he tries, can change for the better. Prison can help people get off drugs or stop drinking or become educated. People can also get counseling in prison and learn how to handle their feelings better.

Your brother going to prison has changed your family. It's not easy for anyone. But you're a family, you can be strong together, you can love each other, help each other, and get through hard times together.

Good luck to your brother, good luck to your family —and good luck to you!

Sometimes prison can be a turning point for a person, so that he changes his life and makes it better. In the story, Chris is determined to make his family proud.

Questions to Think About

1. What are some of the things that happen in a family when someone they love gets sent to prison?

2. How can people in a family help each other during this time?

3. What are some of the things a kid can do to stay in touch with a family member in prison?

4. If someone in your family was in prison, what would you hope would be different about them when they got out?

Further Reading

Bender, Janet. *My Daddy is in Jail: Story, Discussion Guide, and Small Group Activities for Grades K-5*. Chapin, SC: YouthLight, Inc., 2003.

Bernsten, Nell. *All Alone in the World: Children of the Incarcerated*. New York: The New Press, 2005.

Martone, Cynthia. *Loving Through the Bars: Children with Parents in Prison*. Santa Monica, Calif.: Santa Monica Press, LLC, 2005.

Walker, Jan. *An Inmate's Daughter*. Norris, Mont.: Raven Publishing, Inc., 2006.

Woodson, Jacqueline. *Visting Day*. Scholastic, Inc., 2002.

Find Out More on the Internet

The Center for Children of Incarcerated Parents
www.e-ccip.org

Children's Justice Alliance
www.childrensjusticealliance.org

Family & Corrections Network
fcnetwork.org

Prisoners of Love
www.prisonersoflove.com

S.K.I.P. Inc.
www.skipinc.org

The websites listed on this page were active at the time of publication. The publisher is not responsible for websites that have changed their address or discontinued operation since the date of publication. The publisher will review and update the websites upon each reprint.

Index

Picture Credits

Creative Commons Attribution 2.0 Generic
    Chan, Eric (maveric2003): p. 35
    Denker, Patrick: p. 38

Dalton, Linda; fotolia: p. 37
photobunny, fotolia: p. 31
photodisc: p. 40
Stewart, Benjamin: p. 43
Zalesny, Jeffrey; fotolia: p. 32

To the best knowledge of the publisher, all images not specifically credited are in the public domain. If any image has been inadvertently uncredited, please notify Harding House Publishing Service, 220 Front Street, Vestal, New York 13850, so that credit can be given in future printings.

About the Authors

Sheila Stewart has written several dozen books for young people, both fiction and nonfiction, although she especially enjoys writing fiction. She has a master's degree in English and now works as a writer and editor. She lives with her two children in a house overflowing with books, in the Southern Tier of New York State.

Rae Simons is a freelance author who has written numerous educational books for children and young adults. She also has degrees in psychology and special education, and she has worked with children encountering a range of troubles in their lives.

About the Consultant

Cindy Croft, M.A. Ed., is Director of the Center for Inclusive Child Care, a state-funded program with support from the McKnight Foundation, that creates, promotes, and supports pathways to successful inclusive care for all children. Its goal is inclusion and retention of children with disabilities and behavioral challenges in community child care settings. Cindy Croft is also on the faculty at Concordia University, where she teaches courses on young children with special needs and the emotional growth of young children. She is the author of several books, including *The Six Keys: Strategies for Promoting Children's Mental Health.*